We hope this book will help

undergoing chemotherapy.

provide additional inner strength

to the people living through cancer

and the families and friends

who love them.

Aloxi
palonosetron HCl injection

Distributed and marketed by
MGI PHARMA, INC. Bloomington, MN. 55437
under license of Helsinn Healthcare SA, Switzerland.
©2006 MGI PHARMA, INC. Bloomington, MN.
55437 U.S.A. ALO188   4/06

A Gift for

_____

From

_____

YOUR *Guardian Angel's* GIFT

Christine K. Clifford

BRONZE BOW
PUBLISHING
www.bronzebowpublishing.com

Dedication

To Harry Beckwith,
who has given me wings,
and to our six children—
Tim, Brooks, Harry,
Will, Cole, and Cooper—
who make us fly.

Appropriately, it happened in the air.

I was in flight. Appropriate, too, it was just before Christmas, when our thoughts so easily turn inward, and then upward.

I looked out the airplane window, reflecting on a year of struggle and

on how I'd overcome it.
And suddenly it came into view:

A feather.

I began to write. And I wrote and
wrote and wrote, and within seconds
it seemed, it was done: this poem,
in the exact words that follow.

That moment was a gift to me.

This is mine to you.

Christine K. Clifford

There's a story

to this feather

Rather simple,

but it's true,

It fell straight down from heaven

As a sign meant just for you.

See,
we all have lifelong
challenges,

Adversity and fear,

Adversity and fear,

Adversity and fear,

Your Guardian Angel's Gift

But your *Angel* up in

Heaven

Sees *every* little tear.

God

chose your

Special Angel

For those times you cannot

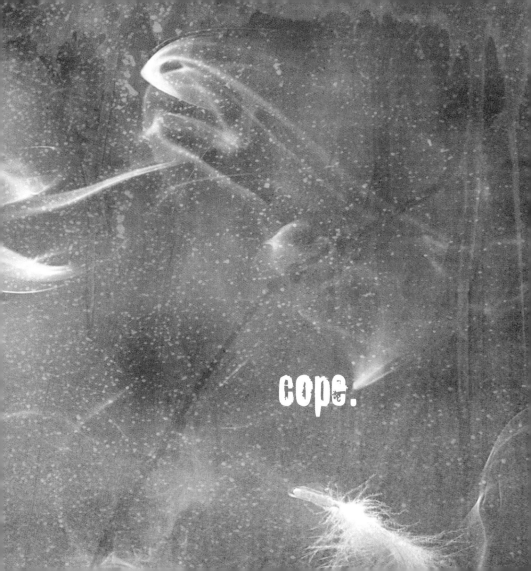

cope.

He put Her there
to let you know,

Don't ever
give up

hope.

If you struggle, fight,

or just feel lost,

You'll always know

She's there.

She sent this feather

down to earth

To let you know

"*I care.*"

If you ever feel you're

stumbling,

Remember: stand up

STRAIGHT AND TALL,

Your personal

Guardian Angel

Will never let you fall.

So if you're ever

FRIGHTENED,

WORRIED,

Lonely,

in DESPAIR,

Remember that this feather

Traveled miles

through the air.

It went through

sleet

and *rain*

and

snow,

Crossed deserts

far and wide.

It tossed about,

turned upside down
upside

but landed

It will always be beside you,

A beacon

in the night,

And every morn as *daybreak* comes,

This gift will be
your *light.*

BEFORE HER BOUT with breast cancer, Christine Clifford had definitely cracked the glass ceiling. At the age of forty, she was senior vice president for SPAR Marketing Services, an international information and merchandising services firm in Minneapolis, Minnesota.

Diagnosed with breast cancer in December 1994, she went on to write four humorous portrayals of her story in books entitled, *Not Now…I'm Having a No Hair Day!*, *Our Family Has Cancer, Too!* (written especially for children), *Inspiring Breakthrough Secrets to Live Your Dreams*, and *Cancer Has Its Privileges*.

Christine is currently president and chief executive officer of The Cancer Club®, a company designed to market helpful and humorous products for people who have cancer. She speaks to organizations worldwide about finding humor and getting through life's adversities.

She lives with her husband, Harry, in Minneapolis.

Check out her web sites at www.cancerclub.com and www.ChristineClifford.com

The Guardian Angel Feather
ornament is available in either
pink, teal, or blue. To order,
visit us at www.cancerclub.com

A portion of each sale is
donated to charity.